Building Wings

John ~~Terry~~

John

To Nikki

with best wishes

for your uni-verse

of Poetry

1-10-2009

First published 2009
by City Chameleon
82, Colston St,
Bristol,
BS1 5BB

ISBN 978-0-9551180-5-0

A CIP copy of this book is available from the British Library

Designed by City Chameleon
Cover designed by Katie Marland
Printed by Short Run Press

Also by John Terry:
Insecurity Report, Driftwood Publications
ISBN 0-9539217-9-4

LOTTERY FUNDED

Acknowledgements

To everyone who helped to add a keel and rudder to this collection and all those who contributed a nail, a screw, a word, or a look:

Heartfelt thanks to Alana Farrell, who initially created order from my disorder and has remained unfazed by my constant additions, revisions and deletions.

The late Linda Lamus, whose friendship and encouragement are sorely missed.

Everyone in Linda's PoetryWorks group.

Philip Gross for kindnesses and his hundred words.

The amazingly attentive audiences at Bristol's Acoustic Night; and (of course) its indefatigable organisers.

Bertel Martin (City Chameleon) who believed these poems could fly.

Thanks also to the editors of the following publications in which many of these poems first appeared: *Acumen, Envoi, Iota, Smiths Knoll, The Frogmore Papers, The Interpreter's House, the North, Rain Dog, Poetry Ealing, Purple Patch, Snakeskin, Wildlife (Avon Wildlife Trust), Peterloo Poetry Competition Anthology. When Pigs Chew Stones, The Machineries of Love, Losing the Edge (Ragged Raven Anthologies), City - Bristol today in poems and pictures, Rats for Love - the Book.*

Dictated while in captivity won the 2008 Pitshanger Poets Open Poetry Competition, The Machineries of love won the 2007 Ragged Raven Press Competition, Stitching mountains together won the 2005 Iota Poetry Competition, Feet in the clouds won the 2002 Ware Poets Open Poetry Competition. Train spotting was placed 3rd in the 2005 Frogmore Prize, South was 3rd in the 2005 Barnet Open Competition.

Foreword

These poems have in common a passion for how inventions affect our perception of what is possible, and a grief for lost and drowned things. Water and voyaging invade many poems, and a trip is as likely to be to imaginary territories such as the world's edge or Victorian Mars as in more everyday places such as around a washing machine. The traveller might be Joshua Slocum, sailing around the world single-handed for the first time, a wife flying south on handmade wings after her husband, or a ghostly motorbike rider, but it is the journeying these poems are about. They question how we know we are going anywhere, and how far it's possible to travel without moving. The collection is both an elegy for vanished machinery and for the people who made it, and a celebration of the way everything has holes in its socks.

Alana Farrell

for Alana

Contents

Fill me up

Fill me up
before I stutter to a halt.
This road
has no layby
or picnic area.

Narrow
twisting
cut into flanks
of mountains
edged with precipice.

Blind bends
rockfalls –
no place to be caught
with an empty tank.

Fill me up:
let's see
how far I can get
before nightfall.

A Crowd of Cranes

They grow in empty places,
tower above bare ground.
Clear a space in any city
and they sprout like weeds
after London's Great Fire.

From the high-up window-wall
of the Mall coffee bar,
I count ten
invading tower cranes
beginning to move
as lunch time ends.

Swinging across the neat
white fields of foundations,
alive with a dancing buttercup
speckle of hard yellow hats.

Each day crane drivers
climb sky-high ladders
to start work.
A good workout, too –
health clubs would charge a hefty fee
to oversee this daily effort;
money is their bottom line.

Not the line drivers see
looking along the latticed
neck-stretch of the jib;
they're getting on with the job –
making it all happen.

Filling up the spaces.

A Child's Garden

Grandma's garden was cuddled by warm
brick walls; its cosy patch
of grass and tidy flower beds

edged with brick, and overlooked by brick-
backed houses. Out in the street
were manholes with iron lids

that were brick all the way down
– as if the whole world was built
from brick, and dirt invented afterwards

so that trees and privet and snapdragons
could grow and never scrape their toes.
I broke a spoon, digging through flowers

to find the world's real foundations.
When grandad dug trenches to bury
the rabbits' old bedding, I was there

in case his spade clanged on brick
and cracked open the roots of the world.
I couldn't tell him to be careful –

his moustache was enough to scare God –
so when nothing happened I asked
grandma how far down the dirt went:

Right down to the centre of the world,
she said briskly, sliding a rabbit
pie into the oven. Her answer was *unacceptable* –

but so were pies made from rabbits
I'd petted and fed until they grew
big as ideas and were gutted by the hard-

handed, grown-up world – but I always
ate the pies; and always there were new
rabbits to care for; fresh ideas to feed.

Papa's Pigeon

              fills the ballroom with outstretched wings
nudging Mama's grand piano into a corner, so she must
dodge wood and fabric in order to reach the keyboard
and always, as she does, her fingers pluck arpeggios
from bracing wires until the biplane sings like a harp.
Half a tone down, she calls, touching the note.

She plays the promenade from *Pictures at an Exhibition*
taking her time from uncle Rupert's leisurely stroll
with Papa as they inspect the machine from wings to tail
– laughs when they stop to argue over a cable-run,
her fingers skipping through the *Tuileries* section,
scattering the falling thirds Mussorgsky wrote
to mimic the voices of quarrelling children –
nah nah na-na nah.

I skip upstairs, put on a dress; beg cook for French
toast and wander back, nibbling and dropping crumbs.
Tiptoed, I can touch the carved wooden propellers –
two slim sisters, each married to an engine
that squats like an iron toad until jerked awake
by its own explosive coughs; dribbling and spitting
discoloured oil to stain our once-perfect parquet.

No one can dance again until Papa's carpenters
have time to replace damaged herringbone
with fresh-planed oak blocks; each matched
to the old and polished with chunks of beeswax.

A scramble from wings to fuselage to reach
the glass and mahogany cabin where Papa
and uncle Rupert are testing the controls. I stand
between them like a captain, shouting *port – starboard,
up – down;* fall madly in love with the joyous flip-flop
of ailerons; laugh and clap my hands to see rudder
and elevators obedient as trained elephants.

Mama is sad and plays Satie,
who died last week in Paris. I will never die,
and certainly not in summer; could not bear
to lose my favourite months –
though even seasons, they say, are different in Paris.

From the keyboard her fingers detach unresolved
sevenths and ninths, building layers of slow chords
that hover over the piano on outspread wings.

Ballerina

It could be a telescope, rising section by impossible
section to peer into clouds; but no, it's a red-painted
mobile crane, with a cab the size of a Portakabin –

a pickup for the French crane that's wowed the site
for months – gracefully pirouetting on one slim leg,
the thirty-metre latticework of her extended arm

no thicker than lines drawn on sky with a sharp pencil.
Like any accomplished *artiste*, she's always in demand,
forever packing and travelling to dance in another town.

Not that you'd recognise her bright yellow bones,
collapsed and folded into a neat package – a kid's buggy
kicked flat by a mum with baby and a bus to catch.

This kid's no baby, and despite her catwalk slimness,
no lightweight either. Takes three guys and a crane
to bed her down in a custom trailer. Two unlock

and fold her triangular feet; the other signals the big
red crane, left hand extended – you'd think
he was hailing a bus, but he stands on latticed girder

dangling on chains, six metres up. He guides and checks
the slow swing; positions her over the waiting trailer;
eases down until lugs align and pins are driven home.

The rest is small details of packing; boring as socks.
Locked to the truck, everything clicked and connected,
she's off to touch base in Bromsgrove; after that – well,

her agent's books are full. She'll dance until she drops.

Cinema Days

Here two projectors
run alternately, side by side.
I rewind ciné reels as they fill,
check and re-splice brittle joints,
breathe the cloying sick-sweet stink
of acetate.

Days are school.
Nights I use staff-only doors,
learn of life behind gilt and plush
– how the projection box at changeover
grows tense as the command deck
of a submarine.

Fire has run
through this cramped box,
the blistered walls still unpainted,
ancient, heat-distorted fittings
still in place beside the new.
After changeover I'm left

to trim arcs in the dancing darkness,
keep the black and white image sharp.
Picture myself on screen
saving the ship. The *Pathé* news
which starts our second half, is shared
with another shabby cinema

the far end of town.
On the bus I hold the film-can
so the logo is clearly seen
– proof of identity beyond schoolboy.
Fifteen, and look! I carry the world's
news in my arms.

The Fires of August

Take a blood-hot evening: add
a sudden huff of dragon's breath
– and empty, sweat-stained air becomes
a silent towering rush of nylon,
stooping like a hawk; a vivid
presence of taut fabric, clawing
for height on fierce bursts of flame –

lifting from its headlong swoop
to clear oak and sweet chestnut,
follow their drop into the valley,
and never shake a leaf, though jays
scream alarm and angry magpies
out-swear the chattering squirrels.

As night drops, hotter than blood,
the grounded envelope still stretches
its defeated dome above our trees.
We stay and watch; who could sleep
when even dragons cannot fly.

Tall Trees are Tall Ships

Too much sail! Can't cut the cables and run
for fear the storm will strip our canvas;
carry away all spars from sprit to mizzen.
Aloft there, you fluttering fools – Jesus! –
Man the yards, or we're aground – keep her going!
You'd swear the keel's grown roots; this shore's a trap
and we're landlocked. Branches crack, broadcasting
autumn's first full storm – and I've been asleep
all summer, dreaming under my own leaves
outspread on wide branches to catch the sun –
the way a tall ship grows extra sails to catch
the wind. Full-leafed, I drove myself through waves,
always my own captain. I wake as autumn
storms me into winter without a stitch.

Opening

Nothing this morning;
except curtains opened on hard frost.

Nothing
except the robin, pecking awkwardly
over one shoulder, perched sideways
on a feeder designed for tits.

Nothing
except a sharp-eyed blackbird and his mate
gathering crumbs from sun-touched grass
beneath the swaying robin.

Nothing
except a squirrel, hanging head down,
busily nibbling tight new buds
from almost inaccessible twigs.

Nothing
except low sun through bare intricacies
of woodland, lighting my quiet room
with all the warmth that winter steals.

Voyager

Twenty thousand leagues under the trees,
so deep in green I could drown –
caught in a seaweed of wind-tossed oak,
chestnut, beech and hawthorn,
where birds swim in and out like fish.

Deep-water sailor, submariner,
I watch sea-leaves shaken by tides,
incandescent as a world's beginning –

my brick-built keel poised two fathoms
above a seabed littered with daisies;
submerged windows angled
against a fingered insistence of waves
whose storms of shifting colour
shake the mind like willow,
burst through watertight glass
and flood my spilt-wine carpet
until plain, painted walls dissolve in light –

burning away months of darkness
fumbling beneath roots of ice
for a course towards remembered seas.

I am Nemo, captain of the Nautilus,
submerged beneath the seasons of my trees.

Dictated while in Captivity

Fifteen days from the coast,
near to the source of four great rivers,
we found a land where men and women
bud and grow like leaves,
living but a single season.

Each branch a family, each tree
a city of multitudinous inhabitants,
crowded with whisper, murmur and chatter –
every leaf boasting individual features
like to ours, though (of necessity)
in low relief, such as Donatello
the Florentine, would need all
his artistry to match.

Of a certainty, they had no souls
and what resistance could they offer
when a few strokes of an axe
might fell both city and citizens?

We plucked upwards of a thousand,
carefully laying them in barrels
with salt between each layer
as one preserves fresh roses.
But being dead, if not yet brittle,
their features shrank to invisibility.
So, for all our contrivance, we brought back
nothing but autumn and the colours of death.

Of the branches we cut, none survived,
nor (despite our skill) would they root in tubs
but cried piteously and shrivelled within a day.
Our surgeon insisted they had language
and made shift to set down their words,
but took a fever and died beneath the trees;
at which his notebook, fluttering unbound,
escaped, and was never recovered.

Landfall
(for Ella)

Exhausted from the voyage
she sleeps like Gulliver, wrecked
and cast up on dry land.

She has none of the words
for dryness; but knows
already the desiccated taste of air;

knows the shock of light
that struck after the wave burst –
closed eyes can't keep it out.

This beach is sand against her skin.
She's lost her world's heartbeat,
the womb's fluid embrace.

In her first breath-taking sleep
she has the look of a voyager,
whose wisdom is a secret

no one understands,
though they come from the same sea.
She will learn their speech,

struggle to translate
from the language she was born with:
draw charts of unimagined oceans.

Sailing Alone Around the World

He navigated by the moon; but wasn't mad –
Captain Joshua Slocum from Nova Scotia:
the master mariner who turned the joke
back on the friend who gave him the *Spray* –
a rotting boat in a Fairhaven field:
...at some distance from salt water.

The field grew pasture oak for keel and frame:
Slocum rigged a boiler to steam new ribs,
and bent them to shape over a log.

He planked with inch and a half Georgia pine,
the butts fastened with bolts and nuts,
and laid his deck on six-inch beams.
It was my intention, he wrote,
to make my boat strong.

Not the man to rely on fancy gear,
paid a dollar for a broken-faced tin clock
that worked better after it was boiled.
With his sextant, the approximate time,
and a set of lunar tables, he could fix
the *Spray's* exact position on the globe:

which other ships confirmed: *Forty-eight west
– as near as I can make it* – cried
a steamship Captain. The thirty-six foot
Spray with her tin clock
had exactly the same longitude.

It lacks but three minutes to the half-hour,
shouted the Captain of the *SS Olympia.*
Slocum felt this man was a little
too precise in his reckoning.
Over-confidence, he believed, sank
the liner *Atlantic* and more like her:
their captains knew too well where they were.

What truth Captain Slocum's lunar tables spoke
was checked against intuition, the patent log,
the experience of a thousand voyages:

From April, eighteen ninety-five
to June, eighteen ninety-eight,
Slocum and his tin clock
wound themselves round the world like a spring.

Solo

Years in orbit –
pointing out to myself
at each pass
the same landmarks.
Tired eyes wide open
as the nightside
crawls beneath.

A closed system
spun about a single centre.
My astronaut's bones dissolving,
adapting to a life
without weight.

Much more of this
and I'll change past return.
Never go back
to feel adapted bones snap
within the rich
gravitational pull
of another body.

Ammonia

It takes more effort now
to see the boy who holds his mother's hand.
I can't see his face, or hers –
must look, as he does,
to where the compressor under the stairs
labours to chill fridges in every flat.
He never moves; hasn't moved in years,
except to grow more distant.

My only certainty is that he's not me.
I'm the ghost whose aura enfolds him
for brief moments. Does he feel me there?
I have no memory of any presence.

But, of course, it's not myself
I invisibly embrace as he stands in the hall,
by the stairs that lead home; wrinkling his nose
against a sharp smell of ammonia
from the compressor I no longer hear.
If his mother speaks there are no words;
time has robbed me of the voice he knew so well.

The slightest whiff used to take me
to that hall, by those stairs.
I believed, then, that he was me;
knew the hand he held was warm. I still reach out
but the hand clasping hers isn't mine
and ammonia has lost its power
over dimensions.

This, then, is the only me
holding a hand out to the dark.

Mud

The twisted thread of shrunken river
needles through thick, folded fabric
of grey mud; low tide's embedded stumps
alive with a white brilliance of birds
racketing between sky and bank.

Screams that focus my eyes – lead them on
from gull to duck to stilted cormorant;
show the forked patterns of busy feet,
the beaked furrow of the hunted worm.

My attention grabs at detail, is caught
by sudden dazzles of reflected light,
stronger than October's slanted sun,
fading sky and birds into background.

Carved by retreating water, mud is art
to burn the naked eye – fierce as gold
from Benvenuto Cellini's furnace –
a tumble of burnished slopes that out-glare
the long, level smile of the other bank.

Thrusting between them, the returning tide
carries a confetti of feeding gulls
afloat on the flood's swift escalator
which drowns all art twelve metres deep –

whose naked ebb will show the river's bed
scoured and creased in fresh complexities.

Invaders

Martians they were – we can't prove it,
but who else would attack
the old railway embankment,
stealing our skyline with their red machines?

I rang the council
demanded infantry, field guns,
a squadron of RAF biplanes.

They said I'd got the wrong movie:
it was *King Kong* who swatted biplanes –
War of the Worlds had more modern stuff.
The idiots rang off before I could explain.

Red earth, red dust –
that's what attracted them.

In two weeks
they gobbled up our embankment
to create a Martian landscape,

left nothing but a broad strip
of raw earth; a view
of gardens beyond ours;
the stare of long-hidden windows.

Invaders
            peering through a twitch of curtains
as if we were exotic lifeforms
from a distant planet.

Mars
(Percival Lowell, 1896)

More than a hundred years since this
faded binding was new, the thick
soft pages uncut. Opened,
Lowell's *Mars* surprises: its arguments
lucid as the well-proportioned typeface –

observation, thesis, synthesis; together
with careful maps which must have delighted
Schiaparelli's careless translators – his
long dark lines traversing the planet
become Victorian engineering

of staggering proportions. Vast canals
slice across continents, channelling
precious water from the poles –
their neatly ruled grid measuring
the struggle to save a dying world.

To inhabitants of a more optimistic era
this was logic, science, and romance
welded into a story which carried
a thrilling hint of Earth's final days.

Our image is lifeless: moon-cratered,
eroded by vanished rivers, smothered
by month-long sandstorms.

No single feature
matches the global web of intersecting
waterways, mapped
by Schiaparelli, Lowell, Pickering –
years of painstaking observation
overwritten by NASA's satellites
and roving video.

We see further,
but are less certain of what we see.
The astronomer's long stare
perturbs the universe
and particles of probability
knock at doors
swung on charmed hinges
which could place us beside Lowell
and Lowell beside us.

Plough

Half-in, half-out of civilisation, moving from the amber
necklace of streetlights into an invisibility
of bushes and grass, you aim a relieved
shower into the denser darkness
where roots must lie.

Already, your night-widened eyes avoid the glare of roads –
September's quarter-moon is sun enough to light the way
across shadowed snares of dips and hummocks
and there's a blaze of lights
across the sky

– that's the Plough; spirit-levelled to the horizon, handle
and blade slung from seven stars welded to the night,
where the Down shrugs broad shoulders free of trees.
You stand damp-footed on dewed grass,
rooted,
       featherlight.

Blueprint

No scuttling creature
on a rock can croak,
with lizard tongue
through lizard teeth,
the unheard songs
that should be sung.

Let's build a heart
to conquer air
– strong lungs,
a voice that knows
with certainty
which songs to sing.

I take a pencil
and invent the speckled
feathers of a wing.

Songs of Levity

The laws of gravity no longer apply
people wear soft padded hats
to avoid denting the sky
and cats,
who never respected the old laws
anyway, curl on clouds. Their claws
make it rain
spherically.

Water has become unrelentingly spherical
frivolously bouncing from bath, basin, and shower
into every room. In pubs, hysterical
drunks cower
from hair-trigger spheres
of floating water droplets. Fortunately
the gravity of beer
remains specific.

The pound has been allowed to float
finally stabilising at fifteen
thousand feet. Remote
Western counties claim to have seen
airborne coins of
various denominations. Areas of Devon
show small change at ground level – mostly pennies.
From heaven.

Shoplifting has become a problem –
the corner delicatessen vanished last night
together with the olive-skinned Italian
Mrs O'Leary fancied. Bright
eyed, almost vivacious, her breath
today smells of garlic, chianti
and amorous
Italian phrases.

Birdland

Imagine a woodpecker attacking a shed:
the same pickaxe rat-a-tat-tat, the beat
from a jazzed-up machine; a rhythmic

attack on our local swimming pool
– *le jazz concrète* perhaps; a solo
with the range (if not the tone) of a saxophone

demolishing all preservation theories
in an applauding roar of dust and brick
– Charlie Bird bringing the house down.

**

Charlie (the articulated heron) sifts
through rubble, his lobster's claw of a beak
methodically hunting out... what?

His stabbing peck snatches a rusty
reinforcing rod, too scared to wriggle –
beats it free of clinging concrete;

swings into a graceful long-neck stretch;
drops it into the tangled pile of petrified
worms and filleted bones of RSJ's.

**

Lorries descend like flocks of gulls
fighting over a crust. By the weekend
only smooth raked earth is left to lie,

and scavengers must fill their bellies
elsewhere, flying up this motorway
or down that. Charlie has flown

as if he never existed. A solitary iron bird
no one seems to remember; eagerly settling
(who'd dare say in vain?) to create another nest.

Winging It

Damselflies are into sex. Whoever said
only birds can fornicate and fly
never watched electric-blue pointers
lock together, stiff with desire,

flicking in from dimensions outside
our own. Their polished compass needles
point at reeds, slip through folded
space; repeat from another angle

a shimmering two-fingered salute
to ideas of decency. A jump-jet
display of aerobatic orgasm
hot enough to make her tail curl.

An inch above the pond, high
on the wild anti-gravity of sex
her tail's tip pierces water –
and a thousand eggs scramble.

Moving the Hive

After a night in Val's ex Post Office van
the bees were clotted on the bare steel floor,
so stupefied by cold we shovelled them
back into the hive, balanced it on the creak
of a rusty wheelbarrow and started across
the field before they'd become half awake.
Val steadying as we lurched across ruts

past scattered Shetland ponies, unbothered
by our presence; though the stallion reared,
neighing, above Val – not to bar our way
(he ignored me) but as if his snickers
were cries of love, or lust, or dominance;
spotting *female*, despite jeans and anorak,
quick as any builder on his scaffolding.

And after we'd set up the hive – one bee
stung through my sock before we finished –
he reared over the returning wheelbarrow.
If we'd told him Val had no time for men
it might have made a difference.

She thought not.
Over coffee, rolling a cigarette,
she sealed and fired the licked paper,
killed the match, and breathed a smoky laugh:
Pheromones. Time I had a bath.

Rain

Each time I woke
it was to hear the hard beat of rain
on pavement and road
earth and leaf;
hollow rhythm on dustbins,
sharp rain-gravel against glass.

All night
rain poured from broken gutters,
tumbled down the stone face of the house.
Drains gurgled
drank their fill
overflowed,
mouths bigger than their bellies.

Beating against the tide,
sails furled in ragged sleep,
I circumnavigated the raging
drum of the washing machine
spinning away my life
trapped behind glass.

Woke to a fresh-washed world,
watery sun through windows.
Lifted a sleepy face
to the fierce downpour of the shower.

I ran with water,
knew how the earth felt
after rain.

Stirring up a Storm

Under the wings a scream of engines turning on –
Rolls Royce teacups whooping up a storm.
Don't stand too close
there's a wolfish, spun howl of full
metal teeth; furnace breath to huff
and crisp you down to bone.

It sure ain't grandma stirring her Typhoo –
they'd gobble and spit her out with a blur of steel,
a burning breath of turbines;
a ringed bite of fangs fed with solid
air by massed ranks of compressor
blades, breathing in.

Each blade carved by need – shapes to turn
any sculptor into stone. Welcome aboard:
our teacups are brewing storms
and what fine teeth they have!   Hear them howl
outside the window, wings on their shoulders.
Tighten your seat-belts. . . Relax.

FeO$_3$

Feed each atom of iron
with three of oxygen
and iron catches fire.

Its red flames give
no heat we can feel.
Fifty years, perhaps,

might boil a kettle
but only if the water
patiently preserved

every calorie of heat –
which just isn't possible.
Cold fire consumes

iron like wood thrust
into a furnace. Wood dies
quickly. Iron slowly.

Perhaps they both scream.
Fortunately
we don't hear that well.

An Unquiet Eye

He lugged a toolbox up museum stairs,
      cursed the last flight, shouldered
through double doors; was hit headfirst
by a stare from the end of the gallery.

Stood among the junk of neglected
display cabinets – a dump
for disused mahogany and glass –
      he knew himself alone

yet was reeled the length of the room
by eyes that brought more life to paint
      than brushwork should – as if
they remembered a shellburst in the Somme
which left no scrap of her to come home.

Even in the dowdy uniform
of a volunteer nurse, the Lady Alice
      (an aristocratic, half-French surname
      faded gold beneath her portrait)
stole his breath. And who was he?

Only a fixer of failed alarm systems
      who looked into eyes too long alone
and welcomed their almost extinguished spark
into his own solitary self.

      The smile that curved his lips was hers.
The feet that spiralled them down a clatter
of unused stairs were his.
      Both shared her cry of joy –
stepping, unprepared, into the amazing street.

Triumph

The neighbours hated his darkened house,
the harsh-lit garage; the brazen voice
of New Orleans street-bands, trumpeting
over and beyond the ten o'clock news.

Coming in from light and noise, he always felt
she'd be there when he opened the door;
only to find again a dead house that had been alive
a moment ago. He'd turn and stumble

along the path; but before he reached the garage,
know again she was there, and run to burst back
into the same stale smell of emptiness. He never
caught it out. The house could not turn back as he did.

Afraid of nothing
she could handle every motorbike he restored,
and hugely pregnant with their first,
had ridden the Triumph to that year's Vintage Rally
alongside his water-cooled Scott;
laughing at the scandalised neighbours.

That night in the tent, both drunk on Scrumpy,
he'd sketched rude cartoons down her thighs
with gentian violet. When the contractions started
she was squeezed, still giggling, into the sidecar
of a borrowed Ariel Square-Four – no chance

to see the amazing drawings beneath her great belly
because Sister took one look and screamed:
Nurse! Wash that off!
Premature or not, Charlie was a lovely kid;
a New York banker now – but then
none of them were ever really into bikes.

He took to living upstairs, leaning roadworthy machines
against the banisters on rugs that grew black with oil –
knocked out the wall between lounge and garage
to bring the Myford lathe indoors, where it corkscrewed
swarf into fitted carpets – hung rows of spanners
on William Morris wallpaper and allowed steel bars
to lounge full-length
on the settee she'd frilled to match a favourite dress.

No sacrilege, not now.
She still rode pillion to the rallies, warm against him
– enough to show she was there. He'd learned not to look back.

Slade

Moved like a cat. Never saw him till he slammed
two and a quarter pounds of rusty steel on the counter.

> *Fix the gun!*

A gravelly whisper that shivered me down to ice.

> *Need me a new gunbelt, too;*
> *powder, percussion caps, ball ammunition –*
> *an' gimme bear-grease to waterproof the load.*

The revolver was a brittle shell of rust,
red as boiled lobster; mainspring eaten away;
double-sear gone to hell. Sad thing to see –
a decent eighteen-fifty-one Navy pistol
could've fetched three thousand bucks, easy.

> *Don't hogwash me. 15 dollars, brand new.*

Couldn't imagine fresh machined brass and steel,
straight from Colt's factory.

> Looked like it was buried for years.

> *Me too,*

said the stranger –
thin lips, face untouched by sun,
pony tail of greying hair,
eyes with an edge like tempered steel.

> *Went right down to skeleton –*
> *guess it took time to work my way back.*
> *How does a man think with an empty skull?*
> *No eyes, just knew my hands felt wrong.*
> *Working from memory I fleshed them out:*
> *nerves, veins, tendons, calloused skin –*
> *hands of a man who uses his hands.*

Strong fingers stroked the gun.

> *Telegraph Sam Colt, tell him to freight spares.*
> *He knows me – from Fort Kearney, west,*
> *I was feared a good deal more than the Almighty;*
> *and the bastards hanged me. Fix the gun,*
>
> *it's killed twenty-six men*
> *and I guess it'll do it my work in hell.*
> *You've no idea how bones can grieve –*
> *they kept my wife away till I was dead,*
> *and I'm Jack Slade.*
> *Goddamn you! Fix the gun.*

Remembering Belfast
– Occupied City

Saturdays I'd walk
from the aircraft factory,
past the docks, the scrap yards,
over the bridge into Belfast
packed with afternoon shoppers.

Always at the edges of the crowd
the staring camouflage, the tense
young men, never still,
their rifles almost casual,
strained faces scanning
crowded pavements.

Among the swirl of shoppers
a man who might pause
in a doorway; appear
at a window, on a roof,
his single shot still
echoing above the crowd
as he moved.

Always moving,
the staring camouflage
the not-quite casual rifles,
eyes quick as birds,
sharp as beaks,
pecking, pecking,
pecking into the crowd.

Belfast
wrenched youth from
strained faces. I remember eyes
that were never still.

Remembering Belfast
– Working Away

The bed, wardrobe and washbasin
left no more than a door's width
of free space between bed and wall.
A wall on which, long ago, some
thriftless fool had mounted a ridiculous
expanse of mirror. You could stay awake,
they said, and watch yourself sleep.

Death row, we called it, our cells
opening onto a thin, endless corridor.
Friday nights I'd find my neighbour
crouched with the door propped open,
ironing a shirt on the narrow
strip of carpet outside his room.
Getting ready to do the town.

Beyond the corridor, over an unseen
Victorian boiler of limitless power
– which sneezed and coughed all night –
a great claw-footed dinosaur of a bath
straddled a vast expanse of vinyl.
Wide-mouthed taps bellowed water
half a fathom deep, to float me
full length, leagues from the shore.

Only in the bar could we move without
damage, stretch without taking our clothes off.
Sprawled easily under the jaunty spotlights
we drank hot Bushmills and water
with clove-studded slices of lemon;
never talked shop; ignored
ghostly tables set for breakfast,
the ice-studded wind from the harbour.

Remembering Belfast
– Building Wings

Harsh with red oxide,
invisible as patrolling soldiers,
the heavy gates
welded from seven-inch
rectangular steel
stand poised to clang shut.
Ready to seal off
strategic sections of road
shopping malls
and whole living streets of small houses.

Quotations from scripture
boldly painted on barns
or any walls that face the road.
Religious poems from daily papers
jostle with centrefolds on factory walls;
family photographs above desks.
Favourite cuttings
flat and tanned from living in wallets
are lovingly unfolded, shared, read aloud.

Inside the factory down by Belfast Lough,
a machine-gun stutter of riveters
echoes among skeletons of great whales
built from seven-inch rectangular steel
aligned to half the thickness of a hair.

These are the jigs where aircraft slowly grow:
beached on land stolen from the sea,
on floors of oil-stained concrete
that lift and fall with each tide.

Unable to forget its inheritance
the land still breathes
unnoticed by common senses
which, half-blind, depend

on flickering readouts for their truth –

while steel wombs,
gravid with pairs of growing wings,
jig to ancient rhythms beneath their feet.
A secret dance, forever out of time
with rigid systems of clocks and double shifts
labouring to make them bear identical twins.

South

At least once a week, every week for years,
she'd kept on at him to clear the garage:
until one day he locked its up-and-over
from the inside and she heard the sound
of hammering, the clatter of metal,
the sudden shriek of his drill; the beaten
echoes of her own fist on the tarnished
aluminium he'd always refused to paint.

The familiar lock rejected her key
as if she were a stranger. He never spoke,
not even to swear, never sang or whistled –
ignored the food she began to leave outside,
tapping lightly on the aluminium,
her fists grown too sore for aggression.

As winter approached she started to beg:
the house was lonely, the garage unheated.
How could he prefer concrete and the Flymo
to their Slumberland, her flesh under the duvet
yearning now as it hadn't done for years –
heart beating like a Bosch hammer drill,
her nagging complaints filed down to trivia.

When all sound ceased on Christmas eve,
and nine hundred and ninety-nine police
forced open the door, they found a pair
of delicate butterfly wings, cunningly
fashioned from junk and pieces of the Flymo
with the word 'Hers' worked into the pattern.
There was a marked chart of migration routes;
and clear evidence that similar wings
had clipped the lilac as they flew away.

After the police had gone she scribbled a note
for the milkman, folded the chart to its first
section, and left the suburbs; flying up
through the gap in the lilac, heading south.

Feet in the Clouds

Her boots in air, she's standing on her head
and sinking deep in mud. I focus field
glasses to peer through the kitchen window –
enlarge her, times fifty – still sinking. A frog
forms in my throat, I leave the can of salmon
unopened and rush out. My anorak

has gone! I take her bright pink anorak
instead; lace boots tight, grab a spade and head
towards her, feeling stupid in salmon
pink in the middle of a bloody field
so muddy one has to hop like a frog.
If I'd seen this mud through the window

I'd have worn wellingtons – that window
is filthy! And whose fault's that? Her anorak
is minus zip – does up with a sort of frog,
or buttoned loop. Can't push the button's head
through the loop, or vice versa... my field
is really the migration of salmon...

I find the opener for the can of salmon
in a pink pocket. Should be on the window-
sill with the field glasses I watch the field
with. Not content with stealing my anorak,
she's calmly standing on her stupid head
in mud and expects ME... If I had a frog

each time I dug her out, I'd have a frog
farm! It drives me mad. Give me salmon
any day, leaping across the fields, heads
high – I've watched them from the kitchen window
many times; or perched up a tree, anorak
tight-zipped. 'Perched' was a joke – my field

is boring, after all – watching a field
day after day. Rather be a bloody frog.
No one steals a frog's favourite anorak –
because they don't wear them – nor do salmon.
When I've dug her out she'll clean that window:
that's the agreement. She cleans; I save her head.

Then we'll eat field mushrooms and canned salmon,
catch flies for her frog, gaze through the window
at stars, swap anoraks; scrub her filthy head.

Bluebeard's Castle

The Lady Chloe – my latest wife, determined
to infest every corner of the castle, has discovered
a forbidden door, impenetrable as her own conceit.

It hums against her fingertips as if wild bees
swarmed to fill a queenless cavern with wings.
Given her infernal curiosity this discovery has taken

longer than I wished. In her obsessive search for keys
the Lady Chloe has never learned that relays and brass
switches may open any door, anywhere in the castle.

She will tumble into the room, discover the sound
of bees is a vibration of copper coils, an excitement
of galvanometers, a hum of thermionic valves –

I have constructed Leclanché cells small enough
to power the body of a mahogany and brass automaton
fitted with my wife's brain. No more mistakes –

earlier attempts with animals ended with sheep
rusting in the fields; my first wives could not hold
a charge and were broken-up for scrap; but now

as my clock tower peals the morning like an orange,
the Lady Chloe, her naked marquetry polished
with beeswax, wakes me with tea. I dream brass

and mahogany; plan improvements that must be made
before I reconstruct my next wife. Already I detect
signs of malfunction – my tea tastes of laudanum,

her carved fingers grip tighter than they should
(I imagine the clumsy idiot's forgotten my need
to breathe) and I never programmed her to laugh.

Stitching Mountains Together

When they invited her for bridge, she went – exhausted
by the coast's appalling heat, and bored with emptying cases
of gin into a more appreciative container.

Two cases were all that mules could pack on the rough path
that snaked up the mountains (the rest were left in the Jeep).
She stumbled behind, hanging on ropes, or harness, or tails,

unable to stand without support; almost (she thought soberly)
like being pissed – a lot of trouble for a card game.
Which it wasn't, of course. A bridge lay broken at the foot

of its ravine; and she was (was she not?) the builder's widow.
(There'd been no sex; just lectures, with diagrams to show
how cleverly his bridges were built.) She'd have gone mad

without booze – now she needed gin to remember. The mules
must descend (At once, please!) to fetch the cases from the Jeep.
That done, she began, (glass in hand) to organise a grand

resurrection of their dead bridge. They slaved at her command
and wreckage rose to span again, stronger than before.
She quickly learned (after the gin was gone) to drink the stuff

they made themselves; agreed to stay. The mules still brought
an occasional case of gin; and eager young men fought
to obey her every wish (could this be happiness at last?)

Soon she was building bridges across every bloody ravine
she could find. All were poems, airily floating above
a frightful fall; an empty gin bottle in each foundation.

Losing the Edge

The world was pizza –
familiar stars nibbling the edges –
before its disc curled
into a sphere.
The earth beneath our feet
        joining like pastry
                round an apple –

           and not one dumpling
        ever wrote how naked edges met
like lovers touching for the first time.

I can make my mark, no more –
must carry in head and tongue
        the feel of earth moving underfoot
        the yawn of waking volcanoes –
memories of my lost land.

              **

        The world stops at our feet
        ain't sure we likes it.
        Fact I'm sure we don't –
        land should join up neat

        not end in vacancy.
        We might walk off the world
        in the middle of a word,
        fall a different way –

        because there's no end,
        no bottom, life, or death –
        our final gasp of breath
        lasting for eternity; no hand

        to help or fling a rope,
        for none would ever reach.
        Just one thing worse –

no chance of rum, or hope
of drink again. Easy,
shipmates, this edge breaks
without warning. We shakes –
need a swig to cure our dizzy.

**

Who can tell what lies
beneath the world's edge? What kind of monsters?
Living creatures have no appetite
for earth and stones, nor mouths of such size
that a half-league will vanish in a bite.

**

Juan de Vasco, their Captain, cannot tolerate land.
Lost his ship on the reefs of a strange coast
and has, during his wanderings,
misplaced the sea.

At the brink he set leadsmen to take soundings
as if Earth were a great ship
wary of shoals. We laughed as line
spun out, fathom after fathom:
> *Never enough string*
> *to catch the sea.*
> *Ask your Captain, ask your king,*
> *who could spin enough long string?*
> *You must harken when we sing:*
> *what we've seen, you've yet to see.*
> *Never enough string*
> *to catch the sea.*

**

Desperate for his lost sea, the Captain set men to build
contrivances of optic art;
beaten mirrors of copper, polished to reflect every detail;

and so inclined, one to another,
that each produced an image of what the other saw,
though it were many fathoms beneath.

Fearing these mirrors might reflect our world into a fiery eye
and some basilisk glare back,
a mob gathered to smash metal and woodwork –
threatened to cage the strangers
on the uncertain edge – as we do with thieves and murderers,
who are left to sweat until the earth gives way.

**

Birds die that wing too far from the brink;
as do rats and mice we dangles in cages.
Needs a man! Said the bosun and when we shrank
made us lower him on ropes over the edge.
Three fathom down he cries: *Haul up, lads, lively now!*
The edge in his voice made us quick, but he were dead.
Surgeon found no sign of what finished him, or how.
    No marks of teeth, neither, he said.

**

I never hopes to see a mule again, nor scale
such mountains in their company, sure-
footed though they be on tracks scarce wide
enough to set a wine flask. This rain be salt,

bitter as sea; so in barrels us old salts
carries water as on a voyage. Salt scales
on rocks like it was snow. Legs wide-
spread, awkwardly astride and unsure

above the mules' crabbed footwork; sure
of nothing but the chafe of half-dried salt
between clothes and skin – us reaches a wide
shelf and looks down. No man could scale

those rocks to reach a brink that outscales
any waterfall. No matter – we'm damn sure
no ship could live in sea rushing its wide
torrent over an edge leagues across – the salt

spray makes guess unsure – seasoned old salts
we be; but the scale's too vast; the edge too wide.

**

The air was full of humming, a deep bass
that tickled your guts and set the mayor's
gold chain jingling, link against link,

as thrumming ropes inched our town back
from the creeping Edge; quivering the massive
winches anchored high upon the slopes.

A harp laid flat, said Father Ignatius
as he blessed new cordage; a harp with a thousand
wrist-thick strings, each tuned to the same

hellish note and tight enough to burst –
as they do, far too often, gathering souls
in their whipcrack. A town's too much for hemp.

We lost the Cathedral years ago:
destroyed when the undermining Edge
outran our ropes. Foundations crumbled

until aisle and buttress hung far beyond
redemption; and all that great mass
swung past balance, tumbling as it fell.

By God's Grace our winches held.
Men strained all day with crowbars
for each reluctant click of the pawls.

We thought of nothing but gaining ground;
never dreamed the world would change
when Genoese madness became truth.

A haze of land filled the empty horizon,
its green wave hurled in a headlong rush
of hills and wooded valleys. We saw it

leap towards us; felt raw-edged earth
touch and weld in one brief shock.
Our web of ropes tangled and burst

into particles of dust. Pulleys flew apart;
winches spun backward, flinging broken men
broadcast. Silence swarmed like bees.

Our town sat calm on sunlit land stretching
further than we could see. There was no Edge.
Father Ignatius made the sign of the cross
against our new, curved horizon.

Tomorrow, he said, gathering up the oils
to take to the dying; tomorrow we will start:
this town's been too long without a Cathedral.

Strong Steam
(Penydarren, 21ˢᵗ February 1804)

Trevithick wrenched steam from Watt's
unyielding grip.
Made it breathe power –
blew away ninety years
of slow asthmatic breath,
the ponderous nod of great beams.

At Penydarren
strong steam pulled ten tons,
five wagons; seventy excited men
scrambling to cling to the trucks,
or squat, singing, on the iron load
as though this were Eisteddfod,
their dogs leaping and yelping alongside
all the way from Merthyr to Abercynon.

Ten miles in four hours
along a tramway built for horses;
sweating to fell trees and shift rocks,
making way for the boiler's swollen bulk,
the flywheel's spinning blur –

dodging the cross-head that tromboned
forty times a minute between its guides,
the world's first locomotive leaping nine feet
at every stroke, cast-iron track cracking
like dry spaghetti beneath its wheels.

Twenty years too soon
for the easy strength of cheap wrought-iron rails
Stephenson laid from Stockton to Darlington.

Built to settle a bet
Trevithick's travelling engine
was a great wonder for more than a week.

The men of iron took away its wheels,
set it to useful work – bolted down
to drive a hammer.
There was no money in novelty.

Train Spotting

Centre Court darling, Piccarina Gonzales,
still riding high on substances that screwed-
up her third Wimbledon season
and trailing paparazzi like a scarf,

found her stoned self on a railway bridge
where drunken laughter slipstreamed into long
tadpoles of colour, as tough tee-shirts hurled
stolen tins of paint at Intercity trains.

Her first missile, a paint-soaked tennis ball,
skittered and slid across a carriage
doing more than eighty miles an hour.
A wild, amateurish teardrop streaking

across windows and neat livery.
She hit the next express from the trackside –
a fierce forehand from her competition-
strung, hyper-carbon, titanium racquet.

It took six trains to perfect her technique,
to find the critical angle that left
a perfect spot printed on high-speed sides –
the ball rebounding from its brief impact

to hiss a wicked path through rough grass,
scything eager paparazzi to their knees.
The press screamed that Piccarina Gonzales
had just invented the perfect off-court sport –

and Sky agreed prime-time fees to screen
her choreographed tennis teams, strung out
beside miles of track, printing Rolling Stones
lyrics in dot-matrix along both sides

of a speeding Virgin. The tough tee-shirts,
scorning racquet skills, abandoned the bridge
and went back to torching stolen cars – leaving
train spotters space to spot unspotted trains.

Moments

Magic has no place in science.

Take moments –
    scientific moments –
        any of them:

Weight times distance
gives the turning moment of each child
about the pivot of a see-saw;
determines the balance of old-fashioned scales.

You can do it in foot-pounds.

No magic in that.

Or you can do it in Newtons –
that bizarre *Système International* unit
which weighs about the same as an apple

and has an incestuous relationship
with *Joules, metres,* and *kilogrammes.*

So that a Newtonian apple,
rolling off your kitchen worktop,
hits the floor with a force of one *Joule.*

It's still weight multiplied by distance
and even if scientists insist that weight is force

there's still no magic in that.

But once:
a whole orchard of Newtons
(multiplied by sexual proximity)
produced the first unscientific moment.
And the world shuddered under a force of one Eve.
Now that was magic...

Contraptions

'The woman I believed to be my mother
cries for an unknown soldier' – Linda Lamus

The man I believed was my father
cried over the woman I called mother
each time she left him, taking her easel
and paints to prove she wasn't coming back.

The man I believed was my father
believed he was an inventor, and made
odd devices and strange machines
from scrapyard junk and the contents of skips.

The woman I called mother called them
contraptions; damaging in one word
the makeshift construction they'd built together,
which only worked until a remark
wrongly taken, or a misplaced smile,
wrecked some fragile part beyond repair.

The man I believed was my father
carried these failures into his workshop.
A crackle of welding would glare purple
against our windows; while the woman
I called mother painted pictures so dark
they stole light from every room.

Their potential thunderstorm
filled the air until it hurt to breathe
and our cat refused to come in –
eyes fixed on an invisible presence
just behind my left shoulder,
and I'd put her dish out in the shed.

It was the only dish not smashed
when the storm broke and the woman
I called mother disappeared in a taxi.

The man I believed was my father
cried with the woman I called mother
each time she came back; tears that eased
their delicate contraption back to life.

For a while, the woman I called mother
and the man I believed was my father
would be busy inventing new kindnesses
to please each other. Two dedicated
inventors, still attempting to redesign
their machinery of impossible love.

The Machineries of Love

      Visitors to their house would ask:
What use is it? What does it do?
She never said why or how her husband
worked. She knew

      that explanations bred more questions;
would not squander carefully rationed
strength to meet blank stares, or deflect
comments that lessened

      him. They thought their incomprehension
normal; therefore (of course) he was not.
After her operation she'd sat from choice
on a thrown-out

      armchair in the garage, warmly wrapped
in her shawl of drugs, applauding each new part
he created to feed the machine's slow growth.
Was still there; heart

      leaping at his whispered: *Watch!*
As crafted metal began to move in ways
she'd never imagined; or dreamt were possible.
Could never say

      why it made her cry, or how such joy
could come from light just beyond eyeshot.
If he'd been a gardener he might have given
flowers in pots,

      vases of cut blooms in every room;
but nothing she'd like better, or love
more than this machine which had no purpose
but to exist for her, and move

in an interesting way; the only gift
his skill could give; and when at last, unable
to leave the house, she missed the bright
tumble

of its movements, he re-erected it indoors
where she could always see it; locked the garage
and spent his time with her; finding strength
to support her courage.

Long afterwards, convinced that something
of her lived on within spindles and trains of gears,
he built new parts; began to extend the machine,
make it large enough to hide the tears

which still caught him. He ripped up floors
and tore out joists, making room for iron frames
that would guide and support his great design.
Walls came

down brick by brick to allow access.
Simpler in the end to let the growing mechanism
support the house it was devouring; always hungry
to become...

II

High as a church, the Great Machine
naked and complex as uncased clockwork,
dominates Tate Modern's Turbine Hall.

Driven by a voice he still can hear
the artist works alone, fettling castings
until their gritted dust impregnates
a workbench already grained with oil.

Overhead, crowds fill the walkways
where moving parts of sculpted metal
(that fingers ache to touch) twist and dance,

radiant with reflected light, like angels
whose movements illustrate perfection.

They queued until midday to get this far:
well worth the wait – but it's far too much
for one visit –
        each level of the Great Machine
displays a different motion of balanced steel
that thrills the eye as music does the ear.

Critics, who wandered these walkways for a week,
still argue how their feelings of all-enfolding joy
could be built into spindles, shafts and trains of gears.

      The artist works behind a plate glass wall
      where visitors can stare and leave their smear
      of hands, mist of eager breath.

      The glass is polished every day,
      inside and out, but cleaners never go
      where lathe and drill spit coils of biting swarf;
      where iron, rough-cast in sand, is stacked in heaps
      and steel bars crowd in corners of the wall.

His workshop's called *The Studio* now; but not
by him, who conceived and built this masterpiece
which draws so many people every day
to crowd his plate-glass wall like moths

      – the final exhibit and none too soon:
a long day for kids forbidden to run
and parents, arms weighed down with toddlers,
abandon dreams of cushioned settees
and settle on the vast floor.

      The artist works, unheeding. For her alone
      new sections of the Great Machine
      take shape upon his bench.

The Woodscrew Collector

He'd beg the unaccountable spare
from an IKEA flatpack –
a *zinc-plated chipboard Pozidriv* –
but wouldn't steal
cheat, or lower his standards.

Friends tried not to insult him
with anything used, or with a trace of rust –
a worn *slotted-head plain steel countersunk*
could hardly join an immaculate collection
unsullied by screwdrivers.

His method, as far as they could tell,
was to roam streets at random –
looking by not looking.

Disciplined to expect failure
he never dared hope
for a *Phillips bugle-head, non-jamming
collated drywall with phosphate finish.*

Each find seemed more wondrous for being unsought –
a common *Black-japanned, slotted round-head*
filled him with joy; justified the empty weeks
since the *Tapered shank solid brass countersunk.*
The sort of man who could dine on a single potato chip
and think a second would be gross.

For twenty years he gathered screws
as if they were grains of gold:
Corrosion resistant Decking...Double hardened twinthread...

A builder, loading his van, discovered him
seated on a wall, admiring his latest find –
a *Stainless steel security clutch-head,*
and impulsively gave him a cardboard box
containing two hundred, brand new
Reduced shank black-oxide Powerdrives.

And he cried, as if his dearest love had died.

Silences

Rare, but not yet extinct;
brief periods of silence
still exist
and may be tracked down and captured
with patience and a sensitive microphone.

A good capture is more
than unresonating air:
it contains the wound-down
particles of Before –
or the barely perceptible,
anticipatory, tip-toed
movement towards an After.

(Sometimes both, as in the moment
between the end of a well-told joke
and the laughter.)

Shocked, stunned, and pregnant
silences are recommended for the beginner
– leave the more elegant
            until you can extract

at least three levels
of insubstantiality
from each nanosecond
of dead air.

By then you'll be reading the magazines
and acquiring the latest equipment
to explore the silences
present in all speech.

You will also have learned
to ignore the words between them.

The Eighth Day

They gave us motor-cars,
computers, mobile phones
and tiny music machines
neat as fingernails.

They built automatic factories
to make these things
and set them going.

And we so liked
our new shiny world
that it was Saturday night

before anyone missed
the rainforests and the ice caps
and the polar bears.

We blamed the scientists,
the engineers and architects,
and made sure

that not many were left
to work their evil on Monday.
Or the next Monday.

Or the Monday after that.

And although everyone
went on turning ignition keys,
more and more cars failed to start;

fewer and fewer computers booted up,
and no matter how many buttons we pressed
the music just didn't play.

Everything has Holes in its Socks

Everything John Babbington-Mill invented
had been invented before.

He believed there were faults in everything
and that everything needed inventing again –

and Babbington-Mill's re-invented coffee really did
taste rich as the smell of roasting beans.

His re-invented books turned their own pages
and could be read in the dark.

It proved impossible to disinvent war –
but he did invent bullets which said, 'Sorry!'

His incredible Constant Credit card
proved to be amazingly popular

together with the Everlastingly Full purse
that could never, ever, run out of money.

The government said this was treason
and invented a billion year jail sentence,

but knowing there were faults in everything
John Babbington-Mill rewrote his sentence

and escaped in a heavier-than-air, steam-driven
aerial flying carriage – re-invented as a time machine –

which returned empty, except for a brief note
on a recycled postcard: *Arrived back in time*

just in time to correct the faults in everything –
I expect you'll find a few changes when I get back.

Under Ringing Girders

Under ringing girders
morning din pitches
voices to shout
above the roared
words of machines
that foam a tangled
candyfloss of swarf
between their freshly
sharpened teeth
spewing snarled coils
and fragments of steel
dribbled with a milky
froth of cutting oil.

Screaming with rage
they eat down to the smooth
gleaming bones of castings
forgings
bars and rods
and never stop
never lose their hunger
but glare from bloodshot eyes
demanding more.

So ravenous
they will snatch and eat
fingers from a careless hand
and swallow the blood.

How Many Fingers am I Holding Up?

He knew a safe distance when he saw it;
had seen the last dying turns of a lathe
screw off a finger
impatient to check a fresh-cut thread;
always said: *They're stronger than us.*

He'd seen a woman scalped:
long hair caught by a drill spindle
when her cap slipped:
A spinning shaft picks up anything.

> I remember my shock
> when the foreman tightened
> a milling cutter in the Clarkson chuck
> with his two remaining fingers.

> Twice, I misjudged weight:
> lifted and swung too low –
> fingertips crunching between steel and bench.
> The nails turned black and fell off
> – at least they grew again.

But tricked by the false horizon
of new bifocals, my father
had thrust his right index finger
into the hungry wheel
of a surface grinder.

He'd tamp tobacco into his pipe
with the nailess stub; pat
my pockets for matches.
Could never find his own –
even the giant kitchen-box
we bought for a joke.

Gus Garnett

If we needed a tapered mandrel
to grind the latest batch of bushes,
they'd send me to Gus

– master of the Holbrook precision lathe.
He'd slide a length of steel in the collet,
face both ends;

machine a protected centre in each,
and before I could blink, set it spinning
between centres.

Is that right? He'd demand, not looking at me;
tap the compound-slide to set the taper;
take a roughing cut:

Well, it's near enough, he'd tell himself,
making a magician's pass with his micrometer:
We don't want it near

   enough, we want it right! He'd set
the cross-feed and take a single cut:
But it is right!

– and drop the gleaming, still-warm
mandrel into my hand. I'd try the bush,
which always came to rest

(as it should) exactly half-way along.
And finally accepting his own casual skill
Gus would say:
Well, that's near enough then.

Measurement

What's that?
 It's a one-inch micrometer.
What does it do?
 It measures thickness
– third finger
holds the frame against
your palm, index
and thumb rotate the spindle.

Try a hair
nipped lightly between
the anvils – see?
Exactly four thou'.
What's that in metric?
About a tenth of a millimetre.
*It's all battered,
is it really accurate?*

It got in the way
of a milling cutter – my father
straightened it up;
made himself a cast-iron lap
with a precision-ground
twelve-and-a-half thou' step.
Spent hours
lapping the anvils on the high

step, then the low –
a half-turn of the spindle
each time
until both faces were true
and he could set
the barrel back to zero
– there's a special spanner
to take up wear –

Amazon do digital ones now...

Swarf

Gripped in the lathe's three concentric jaws
the rough steel bar
spins to a blur;
steadies to an eccentric outline
ghosting beneath harsh fluorescents.

Your hand, resting on smooth steel,
lifts the polished feed-lever
to start the cut.
A bright ring forms and lengthens
under the advancing tool;
becomes a fresh-cut cylinder
a polished image of stillness
solid beneath the lights.

The moving tool peels away
a rushing ribbon of steel, slithering
hot over the smoking edge, a tight
corkscrewed coil of swarf.
A jagged thorn-stem
twining for support, reaching for fingers
twisting to coil around wrists.

Chained to the cut, you dodge
the jagged whip of heat-blued swarf
writhing towards you;
your hand resting on steel
warming the polished feed-lever.
Wrist poised for the double flick
that snaps the feed off
and on again, so swiftly
that the cut barely falters;
but the jagged thorn-stem
is pruned at source
instantly pushed aside by the new,
jerking as it falls
to join the rustling mass

snarled in the pit
beneath the lathe-bed.

You follow the advancing cut;
watch as the tool's steady logic
skins the bar to its concentric bone;
pilot its approach to the half-seen reef
of spinning chuck-jaws.

And as the fresh coil grows
you carry on
turning to tolerance.